SRA **Specific Skill Series**
for Language Arts

Spelling

Leveled Books
in Nine Key
Language Arts Skill Areas

SRA
Columbus, OH

The McGraw·Hill Companies

Cover: ©PhotoDisc/Getty Images, Inc.

SRAonline.com

SRA

Send all inquiries to:
SRA/McGraw-Hill
8787 Orion Place
Columbus, OH 43240-4027

Printed in the United States of America.

ISBN 0-07-601713-3

3 4 5 6 7 8 9 RHR 15 14 13 12 11 10

GENERAL INFORMATION ON SPELLING

The most recent studies in spelling development have shown that students do not learn to spell by memorizing word lists, as in the past. Rather, students become competent spellers by learning spelling concepts, patterns, rules, and exceptions to those rules. The chart below lists strategies that can help students learn to spell. With practice, students can learn when it is appropriate to employ the different strategies to help them spell most English words.

Sound Pattern Strategies	Structural Pattern Strategies	Meaning Pattern Strategies
Pronunciation Visualization Consonant Substitution Vowel Substitution	Conventions Strategy	Family Strategy Meaning Strategy Compound Word Strategy Foreign Language Strategy Proofreading Strategy Dictionary Strategy

ABOUT *SPECIFIC SKILL SERIES FOR LANGUAGE ARTS*

Specific Skill Series for Language Arts is a companion to ***Specific Skill Series,*** a supplemental reading program that has been widely recognized for its effectiveness for over thirty years. The two series are designed and organized the same. ***Specific Skill Series for Language Arts*** consists of discrete units of practice exercises that target and reinforce fundamental language-arts skills. Units in both series are presented in multiple-choice format for standardized test practice.

ABOUT *SPELLING*

The scope and sequence for Books A through H of *Spelling* focuses on spelling strategies rather than memorization of word lists. The scope and sequence for each book is located on the last page of the book. Each unit includes

- **rule boxes** that explain spelling strategies.
- **models** in each rule box to illustrate the strategies.
- **multiple-choice exercises** for skills practice and reinforcement.

Four **Language Activity Pages** (LAPs) appear in each book. Each LAP is divided into the following four sections and reviews the skills practiced in the preceding units:

Exercising Your Skill reviews key terms and concepts.

Expanding Your Skill provides mixed practice.

Exploring Language shows how the skills apply to real-world contexts by featuring one of six forms of writing: descriptive, narrative, personal, persuasive, expository, and poetry.

Expressing Yourself includes two creative activities related to the skills. One activity is always a Work-with-a-Partner activity to encourage collaborative learning.

TO THE TEACHER

SERIES COMPONENTS

- **Student Editions:** Nine books in each level (A–H) focus on nine skill areas: *Grammar, Usage, Mechanics, Spelling, Vocabulary, Sentences, Paragraphs, Writing Process,* and *Research.*
- **Placement Test Books:** One book for each skill area includes diagnostic tests to place students in the correct level.
- **Teacher's Manual:** Primarily an answer key, the *Teacher's Manual* also includes reproducible student worksheets and further information on how to use the program, including classroom management tips.

HOW TO USE *SPECIFIC SKILL SERIES FOR LANGUAGE ARTS*

Placing Students in Levels: The scope and sequence, complexity of skills, and readability in Levels A through H correspond to Grades 1 through 8. Students may, however, be placed in any level. For example, in the second grade, a student who needs remedial work in a specific skill may be placed in Book A, an on-level student who would benefit from skills reinforcement may be placed in Book B, and an advanced student who is ready for enrichment may be placed in Book C or higher. *Placement Tests* help place students in the correct level.

Setting: This series can be used for independent study and one-on-one practice sessions, as well as in small-group and whole-class settings. It is also effective in after-school and summer-school programs.

Getting Started: Students must have notebook paper or copies of reproducible student worksheets (located in the *Teacher's Manual*) before they begin working. Remind students not to write in the books. Students may begin in any unit of any book, depending on the skill practice they need, although it is recommended that they begin with Unit 1. As they work through the units, students should record their answers on notebook paper or on the student worksheets.

Pacing: Students should be encouraged to work at their own pace, completing a few units every day or every other day.

Scoring: Teachers should score units as soon as they have been completed. Then a discussion can be held in which students justify their answer choices.

Internet Use: Some activities, especially those in *Research,* require students to use the Internet. Students' use of the Internet should be monitored closely for content appropriateness and safety.

TO THE STUDENT

It is always important to spell words correctly when you write. It is possible to become a better speller by learning and applying spelling strategies.

In Book F *Spelling,* you will learn about spelling words

- by studying the conventions, or rules, for adding endings.
- by visualizing, or picturing, them in your mind.
- by thinking about what they mean.
- by referring to a dictionary.
- by proofreading your work to check for spelling errors.
- by thinking about base words and other words in the same word family.
- by understanding root words from other languages.

After you complete this book, you will know that adding endings can sometimes cause base-word spelling changes.

excite + *-ing* = exciting

slice + *-ed* = sliced

plenty + *-ful* = plentiful

You will learn that you can use the Meaning Strategy to choose the correct homophone to use in a sentence by thinking about what the word means.

You can see the boats **sail** from the harbor.

The miniature boat you want is on **sale**.

You will also learn that proofreading your work for spelling errors can help you become a better speller by making you aware of the sounds and words you misspell most often.

A sailboat doesn't have to sail in the direction of the wind. It can actually sail *toward* the wind. Anytime wind blows across the sails, it creates an airodynamick^sp lift, which contains a small forward force and a sideways force. The boat will manetane^sp a forward force if the sails are trimed^sp, or pulled in, effishantly^sp. The flow of water below the boat also creates a force that pushes the boat forward. The keel underneath the hull keeps the boat from sliding sideways.

Correct Spellings: aerodynamic, maintain, trimmed, efficiently

As you master the skills in this book, you will be able to avoid common spelling errors in your work by using the spelling strategies you have learned.

Unit 1
Conventions Strategy

In most words, when endings are added, they do not affect the spelling of the base word:

treats   calming   louder

- In some words, added endings can cause base-word spelling changes. When a word ends in *e* and the ending to be added begins with a vowel, the final *e* is dropped before adding the ending.

  confuse → confusing   rattle → rattled

- When a word ends in a short vowel and a consonant, double the final consonant before adding the ending. However, if such a word has more than one syllable and the last syllable is *not* stressed, then do *not* double the final consonant.

  wrap → wrapper   omit → omitting   profit → profited

- When a word ends in a consonant and *y*, change the *y* to *i*, and add the ending. However, do *not* change the *y* to *i* when adding *-ing*.

  merry → merrily   carry → carrying

United States Territories

Choose the correct form of the underlined word to complete each sentence.

1. The United States has four major territory.
   (A) territorys **(B)** territores **(C)** territories **(D)** territoryes

2. A territory is a region that is control by a country.
   (A) controled **(B)** controlled **(C)** controllied **(D)** controlied

3. A territory can have a vary degree of self-rule.
   (A) varying **(B)** varing **(C)** varring **(D)** vareing

4. American Samoa, a territory of the United States, is locate southwest of Hawaii.
   (A) locateed **(B)** locatied **(C)** locatted **(D)** located

5. It was thought that a territory would eventual become a state.
   (A) eventually **(B)** eventualily **(C)** eventualely **(D)** eventualy

6. Alaska, a former United States territory, is very small in populate.
   (A) populateion **(B)** populattion **(C)** population **(D)** populatyion

Unit 1
Conventions Strategy

The Bear

7. The brown grizzly bear <u>hungry</u> ate the fish.
(A) hungryly (B) hungrly (C) hungrrily (D) hungrily

8. While some bears spend much of the winter sleeping, many zoologists do not call this sleep <u>hibernate</u>.
(A) hibernateion (B) hibernation (C) hibernatton (D) hibernatyion

9. Polar bears <u>active</u> play in the cold outdoors.
(A) actively (B) activly (C) activelly (D) activily

10. Bear cubs are the <u>frisky</u> and most playful of all bears.
(A) friskyest (B) friskest (C) friskiest (D) friskkest

11. When threatened, a bear will <u>angry</u> attack whatever is trying to harm it.
(A) angryly (B) angrily (C) angrely (D) angrrily

12. Bears have only two <u>enemy</u>—humans and other bears.
(A) enemys (B) enemyes (C) enemies (D) enemmes

13. Bears mate once a year, <u>produce</u> one to four cubs.
(A) produccing (B) produceing (C) producceing (D) producing

14. Bears are found <u>main</u> in North America and northern Asia.
(A) mainnly (B) mainly (C) mainily (D) mainely

15. There are seven species of bear, <u>include</u> the brown bear and the polar bear.
(A) includding (B) including (C) includeing (D) includdeing

16. The Asian black bear can be <u>identify</u> by a white V-shaped mark on its chest.
(A) identifyed (B) identifyied (C) identified (D) identifyyed

17. One of the sloth bear's <u>prefer</u> foods is termites.
(A) preferred (B) prefered (C) preferied (D) preferd

18. Bears are large mammals with <u>heavy</u> built bodies.
(A) heavilly (B) heavily (C) heavyly (D) heavylly

Unit 1
Conventions Strategy

Prehistoric Works of Art

Choose the correct form of the underlined word to complete each sentence.

19. Prehistoric humans spent time illustrate animals and humans on cave walls.
(A) illustrateing **(B)** illustrating **(C)** illustratting **(D)** illustratying

20. Drawing these animals most likely took a lot of concentrate.
(A) concentrateion **(B)** concentrasion **(C)** concentration **(D)** concentrattion

21. Many people have travel to France, which has many caves with prehistoric animal drawings.
(A) travellieid **(B)** travelied **(C)** travellied **(D)** traveled

22. These paintings have been preserve for thousands of years.
(A) preserved **(B)** preservved **(C)** preservied **(D)** preservd

23. Most agree that the paintings were not meant for decorate, but served another purpose.
(A) decorateion **(B)** decorattion **(C)** decoration **(D)** decorasion

24. It seems that prehistoric man closely study animals, especially horses, mammoths, and bison.
(A) studyied **(B)** studyed **(C)** studied **(D)** studyyed

25. Mammoths, which were close related to elephants, were as much as fifty percent taller than today's elephants.
(A) closely **(B)** closly **(C)** closily **(D)** closeily

26. In the caves in Lascaux, France, a passage is total filled with pictures of bison.
(A) totaly **(B)** totally **(C)** totalily **(D)** totaley

27. Prehistoric humans also chisel pictures onto bone, ivory, and stone.
(A) chiseled **(B)** chisellied **(C)** chiselied **(D)** chiseld

28. Archaeologists spend a lot of time figure out when these pictures were created.
(A) figureing **(B)** figurring **(C)** figurreing **(D)** figuring

29. Cave paintings of animals have clarify which animals lived in a region at a certain time in history.
(A) clarifyied **(B)** clarifyed **(C)** clarified **(D)** clarifid

30. One painting of a rhinoceros in France looks like an animate.
(A) animasion **(B)** animation **(C)** animattion **(D)** animateion

Unit 1
Conventions Strategy

Choose the word in which the final consonant should be doubled before adding the given ending.

31. *-ed*
(A) sort (B) propel (C) ally (D) uncover

32. *-ing*
(A) sharpen (B) charm (C) permit (D) nourish

33. *-er*
(A) quit (B) hairy (C) embroider (D) straight

34. *-est*
(A) groovy (B) high (C) final (D) thin

35. *-ed*
(A) lurch (B) deposit (C) borrow (D) commit

36. *-ing*
(A) hover (B) recur (C) worry (D) depend

37. *-ed*
(A) defy (B) rebel (C) compound (D) water

38. *-ing*
(A) covet (B) harm (C) dispel (D) devour

39. *-ed*
(A) marry (B) frighten (C) stitch (D) scar

40. *-est*
(A) wet (B) fast (C) mean (D) tight

41. *-ed*
(A) crunch (B) abet (C) underhand (D) reveal

42. *-ing*
(A) count (B) defer (C) party (D) suspend

Unit 1
Conventions Strategy

Choose the word that you would leave unchanged before adding the given ending.

43. *-ly*
(A) shy (B) frisky (C) wary (D) temporary

44. *-ive*
(A) investigate (B) operate (C) assert (D) relate

45. *-ion*
(A) calculate (B) inject (C) elate (D) distribute

46. *-ed*
(A) dignify (B) ruin (C) ignore (D) prefer

47. *-ing*
(A) influence (B) submit (C) begin (D) accompany

48. *-ly*
(A) casual (B) drowsy (C) healthy (D) clumsy

49. *-ing*
(A) rely (B) type (C) distance (D) cuddle

50. *-ive*
(A) prevent (B) cooperate (C) defense (D) relate

51. *-ion*
(A) delegate (B) defuse (C) contrite (D) erupt

52. *-ed*
(A) remedy (B) organize (C) transport (D) deduce

53. *-ing*
(A) attempt (B) grudge (C) forbid (D) ease

54. *-ly*
(A) stealthy (B) grateful (C) happy (D) reliable

Unit 1
Conventions Strategy

- Some plurals are irregular. The spellings of the base words change to form the plural.
  man → men   leaf → leaves
- Some plural forms are the same as their singular forms.
  One sheep stood in the field. Ten sheep stood in the field.
- For words that end in a consonant and *o*, *-es* is usually added. For words that end in a vowel and *o*, *-s* is usually added. Use a dictionary to check a word if you are unsure.
  potato → potatoes   radio → radios

Choose the correct plural form of the underlined word to complete each sentence.

55. The orchestra was going to play two concerto tonight.
(A) concertos **(B)** concertoes **(C)** concertios **(D)** concerts

56. The violist was going to play two solo.
(A) solo **(B)** soloes **(C)** soli **(D)** solos

57. The game of domino was probably invented in China.
(A) domino **(B)** dominois **(C)** dominoes **(D)** domins

58. Flamingo have stilt-like legs and a curved bill and neck.
(A) Flamingois **(B)** Flamingos **(C)** Flamingo **(D)** Flamings

59. The first earmuff were invented in Farmington, Maine.
(A) earmuff **(B)** earmuves **(C)** earmuffs **(D)** earmufves

60. Wharf are platforms built out from the shore where boats can dock.
(A) Wharves **(B)** Wharf **(C)** Wharffs **(D)** Wharvies

Unit 2
Visualization Strategy

When endings are added to some base words, the base-word spelling and pronunciation change. Often the spellings and sounds do not phonetically match. Therefore, it is important to know what the correct spelling of the word looks like.

- The /sh/ sound can be spelled *ti, ci,* or *si.*
  restriction financial extension
- The /^l/ sound can be spelled *-el, -al, -le, -il,* or *-ile.*
  channel annual tremble peril fragile
- The /sh^n/, /ch^r/, and /zh^r/ sounds can be spelled *-tion, -ture,* and *-sure,* respectively.
  creation creature closure

Art

Choose the word that is spelled correctly to complete each sentence.

1. Paintings and dance are ______ forms of art.
   (A) tradicional **(B)** tradisional **(C)** traditional **(D)** tradicionel

2. It is believed that the art of ______ began during prehistoric times.
   (A) sculpture **(B)** sculpure **(C)** sculpsure **(D)** sculpsher

3. This type of art can show all three ______ of a human figure.
   (A) dimentions **(B)** dimensions **(C)** dimencions **(D)** dimenshens

4. The art of creating buildings is called ______.
   (A) architecure **(B)** architecsure **(C)** architecture **(D)** architeshure

5. The Great Sphinx in Egypt is an amazing ______.
   (A) structure **(B)** strucure **(C)** struccure **(D)** strucsure

6. The music composed for operas and ballets is often called ______ music.
   (A) classicel **(B)** classicle **(C)** classicil **(D)** classical

Unit 2
Visualization Strategy

Airplanes

7. Today many people use airplanes to reach faraway ______.
(A) destinacions (B) destinasions (C) destinashuns (D) destinations

8. While in the air, the pilot is in charge of the overall ______ of the plane.
(A) operacion (B) operation (C) operasion (D) operashun

9. The pilots use instruments that measure such things as air ______.
(A) pressure (B) preture (C) prescure (D) preshure

10. Many airplanes are ______ because they can fly anywhere in the world.
(A) globel (B) globile (C) global (D) globle

11. They fly to Alaska where it is cold or to Central America where it is ______.
(A) tropicle (B) tropicel (C) tropicil (D) tropical

12. The Wright brothers believed that creating a flying machine was more than a ______ dream.
(A) nonsensicle (B) nonsensical (C) nonsensicile (D) nonsensicil

13. When they were boys, the Wright brothers' father brought home a ______ toy airplane made out of paper and cork.
(A) simpil (B) simpal (C) simpel (D) simple

14. As young men, the Wright brothers made the ______ to start a printing press.
(A) resolution (B) resolusion (C) resolucion (D) resolutian

15. A few years later, the Wright brothers decided to open a ______ shop.
(A) bicycel (B) bicycal (C) bicycle (D) bicycile

16. By 1896 Wilbur Wright decided to create a flying ______ device.
(A) mechanicle (B) mechanicel (C) mechanical (D) mechanicil

17. Wilbur based the design of his flying machine on the data of Otto Lilienthal, the most famous ______ flight expert at the time.
(A) international (B) internasional (C) internationel (D) internacianal

18. Much to his ______, Wilbur discovered that Lilienthal's data was wrong!
(A) displeasure (B) displeature (C) displeacure (D) displeashure

Unit 2
Visualization Strategy

Up in Space

Choose the word that is spelled correctly to complete each sentence.

19. Space _____ is how humans learn more about Earth, the moon, the planets, and the stars.
(A) exploracion **(B)** explorasion **(C)** exploration **(D)** explorashen

20. Astronauts wait with great _____ to actually go into space.
(A) anticipashen **(B)** anticipation **(C)** anticipasion **(D)** anticipacion

21. For many astronauts, going into space is living out one of their _____ dreams.
(A) personel **(B)** personal **(C)** personil **(D)** personile

22. Astronauts take great care of their space suits so the suits do not get _____.
(A) punccured **(B)** puncsured **(C)** punsured **(D)** punctured

23. In space, astronauts breathe in a _____ of oxygen and nitrogen.
(A) mixture **(B)** mixsure **(C)** mixure **(D)** mixcher

24. Food for astronauts must be convenient and _____.
(A) nutricious **(B)** nutrisious **(C)** nutritious **(D)** nutrishous

25. To help withstand the _____ conditions of space, astronauts must travel in a spacecraft.
(A) brutal **(B)** brutel **(C)** brutil **(D)** brutile

26. Inside a spacecraft, astronauts are protected from deadly solar _____.
(A) radiasion **(B)** radiashun **(C)** radiacion **(D)** radiation

27. They are also protected from extreme _____.
(A) temperatures **(B)** temperasures **(C)** temperachurs **(D)** temperachers

28. Because they are weightless in space, astronauts often suffer from _____ sickness.
(A) motian **(B)** motion **(C)** moshun **(D)** mosion

29. In order to become an astronaut, you must be in excellent _____ shape.
(A) physicle **(B)** physicel **(C)** physical **(D)** physicile

30. Space suits are made of twelve layers, each with a _____ purpose.
(A) speciel **(B)** speciale **(C)** speshul **(D)** special

Unit 2
Visualization Strategy

Believe It or Not!

31. Some _____ people believe that walking under a ladder will bring bad luck.
(A) superstlcious **(B)** superstisious **(C)** superstishus **(D)** superstitious

32. Others believe that a rabbit's foot in your _____ will bring good luck.
(A) possestion **(B)** possession **(C)** possescion **(D)** posseshun

33. Still others think that these types of beliefs are not _____.
(A) practicel **(B)** practicil **(C)** practical **(D)** practicle

34. Most scientists believe that there is nothing _____ about such beliefs.
(A) factual **(B)** factuel **(C)** factuil **(D)** factuile

35. Some people have the _____ that Friday the thirteenth is very unlucky.
(A) nosion **(B)** notian **(C)** notion **(D)** noshun

36. One scientist named Dr. Simo Nayha of Finland decided to test the _____ Friday the thirteenth is unlucky.
(A) proposel **(B)** proposle **(C)** proposil **(D)** proposal

37. He studied the number of _____ traffic accidents on forty-three Friday the thirteenths and more than a thousand other Fridays.
(A) fatal **(B)** fatil **(C)** fatel **(D)** fatile

38. He found that people in Group A had a much higher risk of being involved in an accident on Friday the thirteenth in _____ to people in Group B.
(A) relasion **(B)** relatian **(C)** relation **(D)** relacion

39. He made the _____ that it is only belief that causes bad things to happen.
(A) assercion **(B)** assertian **(C)** assertion **(D)** assertsion

40. Group A in Finland was twice as likely as Group B to be treated for _____ disorders.
(A) mentle **(B)** mental **(C)** mentil **(D)** mentul

41. So maybe, Dr. Nayha proposed, people in Group A had increased _____ on Friday the thirteenth, which is what actually put them at greater risk.
(A) apprehention **(B)** apprehencion **(C)** apprehenshun **(D)** apprehension

Unit 2
Visualization Strategy

The /s/ sound can be spelled many different ways. At the beginning of words, the /s/ sound can be spelled *s, c,* and *sc.* When the letter *c* has the /s/ sound, it is usually followed by *e, i,* or *y.* When the letters *sc* together have the /s/ sound, they are usually followed by *e, i,* or *y* as well.

several | cinema | scene

At the end of words, the /s/ sound can usually be spelled *se, ss,* and *ce.*

course | across | ounce

Choose the letter or letters to correctly spell each incomplete word.

42. The speech was shown on closed-____ircuit television.
(A) s **(B)** c **(C)** sc

43. Although it is mostly peaceful, the brown bear can become quite fier____.
(A) se **(B)** ss **(C)** ce

44. Albert Einstein was a great ____ientist who developed his best-known theory at age twenty-six.
(A) s **(B)** c **(C)** sc

45. If you are at fault in a traffic accident, the police officer may write you a ____itation.
(A) s **(B)** c **(C)** sc

46. Singing voices are classified into several categories, including the ____oprano group.
(A) s **(B)** c **(C)** sc

47. An intense tropical ____yclone in the north Atlantic ocean is also called a *hurricane.*
(A) s **(B)** c **(C)** sc

48. A sharp pair of ____issors is needed to cut fabric.
(A) s **(B)** c **(C)** sc

49. A cutting instrument used to sever tall grass is called a ____ythe.
(A) s **(B)** c **(C)** sc

Unit 2
Visualization Strategy

50. When the moon is less than half of a full moon, it is called a cre_____ent moon.
(A) s (B) c (C) sc

51. Many people visit the coast of northern California for its beautiful _____enery.
(A) s (B) c (C) sc

52. The entran_____ of a castle often has a drawbridge that crosses over a moat.
(A) se (B) ss (C) ce

53. In baseball, a sacrifi_____ occurs when a player gets an out to advance another player to the next base.
(A) se (B) ss (C) ce

54. A _____ensus is a way to gather information about large groups of people.
(A) s (B) c (C) sc

55. When you get a medical shot, you probably win_____ in pain.
(A) se (B) ss (C) ce

56. A painter uses a canva_____ to paint on.
(A) se (B) ss (C) s

57. Another word for great happiness is *bli*_____.
(A) se (B) ss (C) ce

58. An oun_____ of prevention is worth a pound of cure.
(A) se (B) ss (C) ce

59. Tigers wait until the right time, and then they poun_____ on their prey.
(A) se (B) ss (C) ce

60. Another word for a woman's shirt is *blou*_____.
(A) *se* (B) *ss* (C) *ce*

The First LAP
Language Activity Pages

A. Exercising Your Skill

You have been learning to spell words using the conventions strategy and the visualization strategy. Number your paper from 1 to 4. Answer the following questions about what you have learned.

1. If a word ends in *e* and the ending to be added begins with a vowel, what do you do when you add the ending?
   (A) Drop the *e,* and add the ending.
   (B) Leave the base word unchanged, and add the ending.

2. If a two-syllable word ends in a short vowel and a consonant and the last syllable is *not* stressed, as in *diet,* what do you do to the base word when you add an ending?
   (A) Leave the base word unchanged.
   (B) Double the final consonant.

3. When forming the plural of a word that ends in a consonant and *o,* what do you usually add to the end of the word?
   (A) *-es*
   (B) *-s*

4. The letter combinations *ti, ci,* and *si* all make which sound?
   (A) the /zh/ sound
   (B) the /sh/ sound

B. Expanding Your Skill

Number your paper from 1 to 5. Choose the correct spelling for each word when adding the given ending.

1. factory + *-es*
   (A) factoryes **(B)** factories

2. beauty + *-ful*
   (A) beautyful **(B)** beautiful

3. mighty + *-est*
   (A) mightiest **(B)** mightyest

4. elate + *-ion*
   (A) elateion **(B)** elation

5. primary + *-ly*
   (A) primarily **(B)** primaryly

C. Exploring Language

Expository Writing Read the Preamble to the United States Constitution below. There are eight spelling errors. Number your paper from 1 to 8. Write the correct form of each misspelled word you find.

We the peopel of the United States, in order to form a more perfect union, establish justise, inture domestic tranquility, provide for the common defence, promote the generel welfare, and scecure the blessinges of liberty to ourselfes and our posterity, do ordain and establish this Constitution for the United States of America.

D. Expressing Yourself

Choose one of these activities. When you are finished, give your paper to your teacher.

1. Read the definition below. Think of a word that begins with *c* or *sc* pronounced /s/ to match each definition. Write each word on your paper. When you are finished, choose one word, and draw a picture that illustrates the meaning of the word. Label your picture with the correct word.

   Definition #1: one of a race of giants having only one eye, located in the center of the forehead

   Definition #2: a curved, single-edged sword of Asian origin

   Definition #3: a person who is born in a country or who chooses to become a member of a country by law, and who owes allegiance to and has rights and privileges recognized by its government

2. WORK with a PARTNER A constitution explains the basic laws of a nation, a state, or a social group. It also explains the powers and duties of the government, as well as the rights of all the people who are citizens, or members, of that nation, state, or social group. Imagine that you and a partner have been elected president and vice president of the student government at your school. Work with your partner to write a short constitution for your government. Include words spelled correctly with the following endings: *-est, -er, -ly, -ion, -ive, -ed, -ing, -s,* and *-es.*

Unit 3
Visualization Strategy

Common Spelling Errors

Some words you see all the time. The more you see a word, the easier it is to remember how to spell it. Think about how the word looks. If a word doesn't "look" correct, think of the proper way to spell it. Use a dictionary as needed.

Is each underlined word spelled correctly?

1. Many people knock on a door with their nuckles.
   (A) Yes **(B)** No, change to *knuckles*

2. Lunch is a daily occurrence.
   (A) Yes **(B)** No, change to *occurance*

3. The sound of the waves crashing on the shore is very rhythmic.
   (A) Yes **(B)** No, change to *rythmic*

4. A sargent is the rank above a corporal in the army.
   (A) Yes **(B)** No, change to *sergeant*

5. Speaking in front of a large group of people can be very embarrassing.
   (A) Yes **(B)** No, change to *embarassing*

6. Police dogs thoroughly sniff out a particular area trying to find a certain scent.
   (A) Yes **(B)** No, change to *thurowly*

7. Kahkis are tan-colored pants.
   (A) Yes **(B)** No, change to *khakis*

8. Alaskan waterways produce a lot of sammon.
   (A) Yes **(B)** No, change to *salmon*

9. There were a thousand solemn faces at the funeral of the governor.
   (A) Yes **(B)** No, change to *solem*

Unit 3
Visualization Strategy

10. The gladiators battle in the colisseum.
(A) Yes (B) No, change to *coliseum*

11. Basic mathmatics includes the study of addition and subtraction.
(A) Yes (B) No, change to *mathematics*

12. A tornado has terrific winds that can exceed 300 miles an hour.
(A) Yes (B) No, change to *teriffic*

13. A mirage is an optical illusion that makes it seem like there is water ahead.
(A) Yes (B) No, change to *miraje*

14. Soldures in the army must go through basic training.
(A) Yes (B) No, change to *Soldiers*

15. After running a marathon, a runner may feel very egzosted.
(A) Yes (B) No, change to *exhausted*

16. Basil and oregano are erbs.
(A) Yes (B) No, change to *herbs*

17. After being in the cold for an hour, I felt numness in my fingers.
(A) Yes (B) No, change to *numbness*

18. A nome is a small, dwarflike character often found in folklore.
(A) Yes (B) No, change to *gnome*

19. A wedding is a happy occasion.
(A) Yes (B) No, change to *ocassion*

20. The letter to the editor was anonymous.
(A) Yes (B) No, change to *anonimous*

21. The angry tiger nashed his teeth.
(A) Yes (B) No, change to *gnashed*

Unit 3
Visualization Strategy

The Hyena

Is each underlined word spelled correctly?

22. Many people can recognize the <u>wierd</u> cackle of the hyena.
(A) Yes **(B)** No, change to *weird*

---

23. The brown hyena <u>receives</u> government protection from being hunted.
(A) Yes **(B)** No, change to *recieves*

---

24. The laughing hyena is the most <u>familiar</u> of all the hyenas.
(A) Yes **(B)** No, change to *familar*

---

25. Its howl, or laugh, can be quite <u>humerus</u> to listen to.
(A) Yes **(B)** No, change to *humorous*

---

26. Laughing hyenas are found in <u>abundence</u> in Africa.
(A) Yes **(B)** No, change to *abundance*

---

27. <u>Several</u> hyenas can be found throughout Africa.
(A) Yes **(B)** No, change to *Severel*

---

28. Some people think the sound of the hyena's laugh is <u>erie</u>.
(A) Yes **(B)** No, change to *eerie*

---

29. The hyena is a <u>competiter</u> of the lion.
(A) Yes **(B)** No, change to *competitor*

---

30. When a hyena laughs, it is actually <u>unveiling</u> its fear.
(A) Yes **(B)** No, change to *unvailing*

---

31. Although skilled hunters, hyenas are <u>scavengers</u>.
(A) Yes **(B)** No, change to *scavenjers*

---

32. Hyenas will eat <u>carcasses</u>, or bodies of dead animals, including the skin and bones.
(A) Yes **(B)** No, change to *carcases*

---

33. Hyenas can <u>hussle</u>, reaching speeds of almost forty miles per hour.
(A) Yes **(B)** No, change to *hustle*

Unit 3
Visualization Strategy

A New Language and Culture

Choose the correct spelling of the word that completes each sentence.

34. Many teachers use _____ to help students learn a foreign language.
(A) repetition (B) repitition (C) repatition

35. They may also use surprise _____ to help students learn.
(A) quizes (B) quizzes (C) quizs

36. A dictionary is a necessary _____ to use when learning a new language.
(A) refrence (B) reference (C) referance

37. Some foreign languages have words that are very _____ to English words.
(A) similiar (B) similer (C) similar

38. Visiting a foreign country is a great _____ to practice a new language.
(A) opportunity (B) oportunity (C) oppertunity

39. It is certainly _____ to learn a foreign language.
(A) worthwile (B) werthwhile (C) worthwhile

40. Some people travel to foreign countries carrying only a _____ on their backs.
(A) napsack (B) napsac (C) knapsack

41. At times, foreign travelers might feel _____ if they can't communicate with their hosts.
(A) awkwurd (B) awkward (C) awkwerd

42. It helps to study the _____ of a region before you visit.
(A) geografy (B) geography (C) geogruphy

43. Many tourism centers offer _____ that list interesting places to visit.
(A) pamphlets (B) pamflets (C) pamphlits

44. Sightseers of Rome's Sistine Chapel cannot help but be awed by its _____.
(A) brillyance (B) briliance (C) brilliance

Unit 3
Visualization Strategy

Learning More about Earth

Choose the correct spelling of the word to complete each sentence.

45. Scientists study today's Earth to learn more about its past ______.
(A) existance **(B)** egsistence **(C)** existence

46. There are many ______ about how Earth was formed.
(A) theries **(B)** theories **(C)** thearies

47. The origin of Earth is a topic of much ______.
(A) contreversy **(B)** controvercy **(C)** controversy

48. Scientists use a ______ of methods to find more about the formation of Earth.
(A) variaty **(B)** variety **(C)** veriety

49. Earth is ______ to continue changing over time.
(A) likely **(B)** likly **(C)** likelee

50. Scientists will continue to work together, or ______, to learn more about Earth.
(A) colaborate **(B)** coloborate **(C)** collaborate

51. Science professors give ______ about Earth's origin.
(A) lectures **(B)** lecures **(C)** lecshers

52. Researchers agree that Earth is ______ 4.6 billion years old.
(A) aproximitely **(B)** approximately **(C)** aproximately

53. The ______ of Earth's surface is covered with water.
(A) majoritty **(B)** majoritee **(C)** majority

54. Earth is almost ______, with a slight flattening at the poles.
(A) spheracal **(B)** spherical **(C)** sphericle

55. Earth has but one ______—the moon.
(A) satellite **(B)** sattelite **(C)** satelight

56. Earth has survived major ______, such as meteors crashing on its surface.
(A) catastrophes **(B)** catatrophes **(C)** catastrophees

Unit 3

Visualization Strategy

Home on the Prairie

57. A prairie is flat or hilly land that is covered almost ______ with tall grass.
(A) entirly (B) intirely (C) entirely (D) intirele

58. The ______ of some of the grass can reach the height of an adult human.
(A) lenth (B) length (C) lenngth (D) lentgh

59. In the summer, prairies can become ______ hot.
(A) extremely (B) extremly (C) extremelee (D) extreemly

60. The pioneers used the phrase "sea of grass" as a ______ of this land.
(A) describtion (B) discription (C) descripsion (D) description

61. Cattails have a ______ to grow near the marshy areas of the land.
(A) tendancy (B) tendency (C) tendincy (D) tenduncy

62. The grasses, mixed with a variety of flowers, create a ______ beautiful landscape.
(A) naturally (B) naturely (C) natrally (D) natchrelly

63. Native Americans acted as ______ of the prairies, taking only what they needed to survive.
(A) gardians (B) guardians (C) guardiens (D) gardiens

64. Prairie dogs live in underground burrows, which can hold many thousands of ______.
(A) individuels (B) individuils (C) indaviduals (D) individuals

65. Prairie dogs may be weak ______, but they live with numerous family members in underground burrows.
(A) individualy (B) individully (C) individualy (D) individually

66. They can cause a great deal of ______ to cattle ranges.
(A) damage (B) damege (C) damige (D) dammage

67. Because ranchers kill prairie dogs, most of the five species are in danger of becoming ______.
(A) ekstinkt (B) extinkt (C) extinct (D) eckstinct

68. Prairie dog mealtime is often ______ by their chatter and socializing.
(A) interupted (B) interrupted (C) interuptted (D) innerupted

Unit 4

Meaning Strategy

Homophones are words that are pronounced alike, but have different meanings and spellings. Some homophones are tricky to spell.

colonel, kernel

Such words are easily confused because the spellings or sounds—or both—are similar.

The tree is a **beech**. It does not grow on a **beach**.

colonel "a military officer"

kernel "part of a fruit seed or all of a cereal seed"

Remember to double-check the meanings of the words to make sure you are using the correct one.

Choose the correct word to complete each sentence.

1. It is polite to say thank you when given a ______.
   (A) complement **(B)** compliment

2. The Sahara is the largest ______ in the world.
   (A) desert **(B)** dessert

3. The Great Barrier Reef in Australia is the largest group of ______ reefs in the world.
   (A) coral **(B)** choral

4. Water ______ do not have gills to breathe underwater.
   (A) foul **(B)** fowl

5. England can declare men to be ______.
   (A) nights **(B)** knights

6. A close friend ______ your trust.
   (A) earns **(B)** urns

7. There are ______ of people campaigning.
(A) teems (B) teams

8. Loud noises can distract people as they ______.
(A) reed (B) read

9. The ______ is crowded with boxes.
(A) haul (B) hall

10. A hotel ______ has much more room than we need.
(A) suite (B) sweet

11. A helicopter ______ no runway when it lands.
(A) kneads (B) needs

12. Use a screwdriver ______ tighten a loose screw.
(A) to (B) too

13. The ______ of an erupting volcano can be amazing yet terrifying.
(A) cite (B) sight

14. Paul Revere ______ a horse to deliver a message to the patriots.
(A) road (B) rode

15. Chameleons adapt to ______ surroundings by changing colors.
(A) their (B) there

16. A remote control is ______ handy; it controls televisions and other devices from a distance.
(A) very (B) vary

17. The ______ about punctuation marks is not simple.
(A) lessen (B) lesson

18. If you bump into a cactus, you ______ get pricked.
(A) mite (B) might

Unit 4
Meaning Strategy

Choose the correct word to complete each sentence.

19. The act of inhaling causes _____ lungs to expand.
(A) our **(B)** hour

20. Have you ever _____ a caterpillar?
(A) seen **(B)** scene

21. *Pasture* is another name _____ a "grassy field."
(A) fore **(B)** for

22. It is said that George Washington was a man of _____.
(A) principal **(B)** principle

23. Some groups in Africa use _____ as part of their language.
(A) clicks **(B)** cliques

24. The _____ in the library are all occupied.
(A) carols **(B)** carrels

25. A decade or so ago, most phones had _____.
(A) chords **(B)** cords

26. The troubled boy asked for _____ from his parents.
(A) council **(B)** counsel

27. Some people still handwrite letters on nice _____.
(A) stationery **(B)** stationary

28. The _____ on the angry man's head was throbbing.
(A) vein **(B)** vain

29. The firstborn prince was _____ to the throne.
(A) air **(B)** heir

30. Farmers _____ corn and oats in early spring.
(A) sow **(B)** sew

Unit 4
Meaning Strategy

Aesop's Fables

31. Aesop's fables put _____ a moral at the end of each story.
(A) fourth (B) forth

32. Some of the characters like to _____ in the other characters' business.
(A) meddle (B) metal

33. The story about the tortoise and the _____ is very well-known.
(A) hair (B) hare

34. Sometimes a character is a _____ for a specific characteristic, such as greed or envy.
(A) symbol (B) cymbal

35. Many of the characters are animals with _____.
(A) fur (B) fir

36. The _____ characters are often disagreeable.
(A) main (B) mane

37. In *The Ant and the Grasshopper,* the grasshopper becomes _____ from lack of food.
(A) week (B) weak

38. The cold _____ has come, and the grasshopper has not stored any food.
(A) whether (B) weather

39. The grasshopper wasted his _____ during the summer, singing instead of preparing for winter.
(A) thyme (B) time

40. In another fable, a lion with a thorn in his paw is in _____.
(A) pain (B) pane

41. Faced with letting the lion suffer _____ pain or pulling out the thorn, the mouse chooses to help.
(A) grate (B) great

42. The lessons taught in Aesop's fables still _____ appropriate today.
(A) seem (B) seam

The Second LAP
Language Activity Pages

A. Exercising Your Skill

You have been learning to spell words using the visualization strategy and the meaning strategy. Number your paper from 1 to 4. Answer the following questions based on what you have learned.

1. Which of the following words is spelled correctly?
   (A) kayack **(B)** kayak **(C)** kyak
2. Which of the following is a homophone for *hear?*
   (A) hire **(B)** here **(C)** heard
3. Which of the following is a homophone for *hole?*
   (A) whole **(B)** holy **(C)** role
4. Which of the following word pairs are homophones?
   (A) lay, lie **(B)** loose, loss **(C)** know, no

B. Expanding Your Skill

Read the sentences below. Some of the sentences are *from* the Declaration of Independence, and some are *about* the Declaration of Independence. Number your paper from 1 to 5. For each blank, choose the correctly spelled word to best complete each sentence.

1. It was _____ for the colonists to break free from Great Britain.
   (A) necesary **(B)** necessary
2. It was the _____ of the colonists that they should declare their reasons for wanting freedom.
   (A) opinion **(B)** opinon
3. The colonists believed that all men were endowed with "certain unalienable" _____.
   (A) rites **(B)** rights
4. "... Among these are Life, Liberty, and the _____ of Happiness."
   (A) pursute **(B)** pursuit
5. One of the main ideas of the document stated that people could _____ to overthrow a government when it became too destructive.
   (A) deside **(B)** decide

C. Exploring Language

Personal Writing Read the letter below from a colonist who believes that the colonies deserve their independence from Great Britain. Number your paper from 1 to 5. For each numbered item, choose the correctly spelled word to best complete the sentence, and write it on your paper.

September 15, 1775

Dearest Uncle,

I am writing to tell you that I truly believe that the colonies should be (1) (seperate, separate) from Great Britain. Most of my fellow colonists are willing to put up (2) (resistance, resistence) if the King of England refuses to grant our freedom. We have tired of his (3) (tiranny, tyranny). We will make any (4) (sacrafice, sacrifice) to win our independence and finally (5) (suceed, secede) from the Empire of Great Britain.

Your nephew,
Miles

D. Expressing Yourself

Choose one of these activities. When you are finished, give your paper to your teacher.

1. Think of an issue about which you feel strongly. Maybe you think that recycling should be required by law or that students should not have to wear school uniforms. Write your own "declaration" stating the issue and why you feel the way you do. Be sure to include words that are commonly misspelled and frequently confused. Use this book as a reference.

2. WORK with a PARTNER Find a partner. Each of you will use an encyclopedia or another type of reference to look up the Declaration of Independence. Carefully read the article, and make a list of all the words you can find that might be easily misspelled or frequently confused. Compare your word list with your partner's list. Did you have some of the same words? Discuss each word and why you chose it.

Unit 5

Dictionary Strategy

Sometimes words are not spelled the way they sound. Sometimes prefixes or suffixes sound almost the same.

- The prefixes *en-*, *em-*, and *in-* mean "in," "to cause to become," "to give," or "to cover." *Em-* is used before words that begin with *b, m,* or *p.* The prefix *in-* can also mean "not." The prefix *im-* sounds similar to the previous three. It usually has a negative meaning.

  embolden **en**close **in**lay **im**proper

- The prefixes *con-* and *com-* also sound alike. They mean "together." The prefix *col-* also means "together."

  confuse **com**municate **col**lect

- The prefixes *ir-*, *il-*, *non-*, *mis-*, and *dis-* also have negative meanings. When they are added to words, they can mean "not" or "against."

  irresponsible **il**legal **non**believer **mis**file **dis**trust

Use a dictionary to make sure your spelling is correct.

Choose the prefix that correctly spells each word. Use a dictionary if needed.

1. The word _____*panion* means "one who goes along with."
   (A) *con* **(B)** *com* **(C)** *col*

2. The word _____*formal* means "not formal."
   (A) *en* **(B)** *in* **(C)** *im*

3. The word _____*laborate* means "to work together."
   (A) *con* **(B)** *com* **(C)** *col*

4. The word _____*equality* means "not being equal."
   (A) *en* **(B)** *in* **(C)** *im*

5. The word _____*content* means "not feeling content."
   (A) *ir* **(B)** *non* **(C)** *dis*

6. The word _____*clude* means "bring together to an end."
   (A) *con* **(B)** *com* **(C)** *col*

7. The word _____*continue* means "to stop or give up."
   (A) *il* **(B)** *mis* **(C)** *dis*

8. The word _____*behave* means "not behave properly."
   (A) *non* **(B)** *mis* **(C)** *dis*

9. The word _____*polite* means "not polite."
   (A) *em* **(B)** *in* **(C)** *im*

10. The word _____*resistible* means "not able to resist."
    (A) *ir* **(B)** *il* **(C)** *mis*

11. The word _____*mittee* means "a group of people who work together on a matter."
    (A) *con* **(B)** *com* **(C)** *col*

12. The word _____*munity* means "a group of people living together."
    (A) *con* **(B)** *com* **(C)** *col*

13. The word _____*centrate* means "to bring together in one place."
    (A) *con* **(B)** *com* **(C)** *col*

14. The word _____*descript* means "not easily described."
    (A) *non* **(B)** *mis* **(C)** *dis*

15. The word _____*literate* means "unable to read."
    (A) *ir* **(B)** *il* **(C)** *dis*

16. The word _____*battle* means "to prepare for battle."
    (A) *em* **(B)** *in* **(C)** *im*

Unit 5

Dictionary Strategy

Some prefixes refer to numbers. The prefixes *uni-* and *mono-* mean "one." The prefix *bi-* means "two," and *tri-* means "three." The prefix *cent-* means "one hundred."

unicycle **mono**tone **bi**cycle **cent**imeter **tri**angle

Some prefixes refer to position. The prefix *sub-* means "under" or "below," and the prefix *super-* means "over" or "above."

subpar, **super**scribe

Choose the prefix that correctly spells each word. Use a dictionary if needed.

17. The word ______*total* means "less than total."
(A) *sub* **(B)** *super*

18. The word ______*tone* means "one tone."
(A) *mono* **(B)** *bi*

19. The word ______*sonic* means "greater than the speed of sound."
(A) *sub* **(B)** *super*

20. The word ______*ury* means "one hundred years."
(A) *mono* **(B)** *cent*

21. The word ______*ior* means "above the average."
(A) *sub* **(B)** *super*

22. The word ______*ceratops* refers to a dinosaur with three horns.
(A) *bi* **(B)** *tri*

23. The word ______*lith* means "a single, great stone."
(A) *mono* **(B)** *tri*

24. The word ______*form* means "always having one form or manner."
(A) *uni* **(B)** *bi*

25. The word ______*sect* means "to divide into three equal parts."
(A) *bi* **(B)** *tri*

26. The word ______*scribe* means "to write one's name underneath, or sign."
(A) *sub* **(B)** *super*

Unit 5

Dictionary Strategy

The suffixes *-able* and *-ible* mean "capable of" or "tending to." They have similar pronunciations. The suffixes *-ence* and *-ance* mean "action or process" or "quality or state." They also have similar pronunciations. Often, if the base word ends in a silent *e,* you drop the *e-* and then add the suffix. This is not always the case, however. If the base word ends in *y,* change the *y* to *i,* and then add the suffix. Use a dictionary as needed to check your spellings of words with these suffixes.

retract + *-able* = retractable
reverse + *-ible* = reversible
confer + *-ence* = conference
rely + *-ance* = reliance

The suffix *-ness* means "state, condition, quality, or degree." The suffix *-ness* does *not* change the spelling of most base words. When the base word ends in a *y,* however, change the *y* to *i* and add *-ness.*

sad + *-ness* = sadness
happy + *-ness* = happiness

The suffix *-en* means "to cause to be or have," or "resemble, made of." If a base word ends in a silent *e,* drop the *e* before adding the *-en.* If a base word ends in a short vowel followed by a consonant, then you usually double the final consonant.

sharp + *-en* = sharpen   ripe + *-en* = ripen   fat + *-en* = fatten

Choose the suffix that correctly spells each word. Use a dictionary if needed.

27. The word *acquaint*_____ means "a person known to one."
(A) *ence*   **(B)** *ance*

____

28. The word *tang*_____ means "can be touched."
(A) *able*   **(B)** *ible*

____

29. The word *height*_____ means "to raise."
(A) *ness*   **(B)** *en*

____

30. The word *irrelev*_____ means "off the subject."
(A) *ence*   **(B)** *ance*

Unit 5
Dictionary Strategy

Choose the suffix that correctly spells each word. Use a dictionary if needed.

31. The word *change*_____ means "can be changed."
(A) *able* **(B)** *ible*

32. The word *comfort*_____ means "having comfort."
(A) *able* **(B)** *ible*

33. The word *permiss*_____ means "is allowed."
(A) *able* **(B)** *ible*

34. The word *convert*_____ means "can be converted."
(A) *able* **(B)** *ible*

35. The word *anxious*_____ means "the state of being anxious."
(A) *ence* **(B)** *ness*

36. The word *persist*_____ means "the quality of not giving up."
(A) *ence* **(B)** *ance*

37. The word *moist*_____ means "to make moist."
(A) *ence* **(B)** *en*

38. The word *defer*_____ means "the act of deferring to."
(A) *ence* **(B)** *rance*

39. The word *adapt*_____ means "can be adapted."
(A) *able* **(B)** *ible*

40. The word *remembr*_____ means "the act of remembering."
(A) *ence* **(B)** *ance*

41. The word *less*_____ means "to make less."
(A) *ness* **(B)** *en*

42. The word *joyous*_____ means "the state of being joyous."
(A) *ence* **(B)** *ness*

Unit 5
Dictionary Strategy

Choose the correct spelling for each definition. Use a dictionary for help.

43. to make haste
(A) hastible **(B)** hasten **(C)** hastness **(D)** hastable

44. the act of defying
(A) defyance **(B)** defience **(C)** defiance **(D)** defyence

45. the state of being silly
(A) sillyness **(B)** sillyence **(C)** sillience **(D)** silliness

46. to make hard
(A) hardable **(B)** harden **(C)** hardness **(D)** hardence

47. the state of being sudden
(A) suddeness **(B)** suddence **(C)** suddenness **(D)** suddenance

48. the state of being frosty
(A) frostyness **(B)** frostiness **(C)** frostience **(D)** frosten

49. the act of disturbing
(A) disturbence **(B)** disturbness **(C)** disturbible **(D)** disturbance

50. the state of being happy
(A) hapiness **(B)** happiness **(C)** happyness **(D)** happience

51. to make less tight
(A) looseen **(B)** loossen **(C)** loosen **(D)** looseness

52. the state of being friendly
(A) friendlyness **(B)** friendliness **(C)** friendlinness **(D)** friendlyable

53. to give heart; cheer
(A) hearten **(B)** heartten **(C)** heartness **(D)** hearteen

54. the ability to face hardship
(A) endureance **(B)** endurible **(C)** endurence **(D)** endurance

Unit 6

Proofreading Strategy

Check your writing carefully for spelling mistakes. Mark your paper with the SP symbol if you find any spelling errors.

Words with the /ə/ sound (the schwa sound) in unaccented syllables can be spelled in many different ways.

circular smaller actor golden bacon ferret visit

Words with the /f/ sound can be spelled *gh* or *ph.*

rough graph

Words with the /k/ sound can be spelled *qu, ch,* or *c.*

bouquet chord mechanic

Use a dictionary if you need help deciding how to spell a word with these sounds.

Read each passage. Choose the passage that has at least one spelling error.

1. **(A)** Most schools have a guidence counseler on staff to help students. The guidence counseler can help students who may be feeling unpopuler or disliked. He or she may also talk to students who exhibit improper behavior in order to find out the reason for the behavior.

   (B) Some students may be struggling with things outside of school. The guidance counselor must decipher their behavior and get students to discuss their issues. Guidance counselors must be capable of dealing with all kinds of situations.

2. **(A)** Today, people grow their own flowers. One use for flowers is decoration, such as bouquets placed on tabletops. Some flowers have sweet-smelling oils that are used to make perfumes. Others are used to create useful medicines. The flower buds of broccoli and cauliflower are actually vegetables.

   (B) One populer flower is the chrysanthemum. The common variety has been chultivated in the Far East for two thousand years. The chrysanthemum is the emblim of the emperer of Japan.

3. **(A)** Chemistry is the scientific study of substances. Chemists are knowledgeable about the composition of substances and how chemical changes occur. Some changes alter the substance physically, while other changes do not.

(B) For example, when water changes to ice, only a physical change occurs. However, when sodium and clorine combine, a chemical change occurs, and table salt is formed. Farmacists must know about chemicle changes and how chemicles affect humans.

---

4. **(A)** A Seeing Eye dog, or a guide dog, is a dog that is specially trained to work with blind people. German shepherds, Labrador retrievors, and golden retrievors make excellent Seeing Eye dogs. The dog learns the geograghy of the blind person's neighberhood and how to properly watch for traffic.

(B) A Seeing Eye dog must react calmly in dangerous situations in order to keep the owner safe. The Seeing Eye dog and its owner have access to almost anywhere they wish to go, including stores, restaurants, and hotels. Seeing Eye dogs are even allowed to attend concerts and musicals.

---

5. **(A)** Hiking is a form of exercise and recreation. Many people like to visit foreign countries to enjoy natural beauty. Experienced hikers will carry a backpack filled with food, clothing, and equipment that will last for several days through foreign lands.

(B) Good hikers knows basick first aid, such as how to apply a tournichet if someone injures her- or himself. Veteren hikers know that the safest way to hike is with at least one companion. It is also important for hikers to have an accurate map and compuss reading skills.

Unit 6
Proofreading Strategy

Read each passage. Choose *A* if only passage A has at least one spelling error. Choose *B* if only passage B has at least one spelling error. Choose *C* if both passages have at least one spelling error.

6. **(A)** Animals have many different ways to protect themselves from predaters. One way is by camaflaging themselves using their surroundings. A cameleon can change colors as it moves, taking on the color of what is under or behind it. This makes the cameleon difficult for others to see.

(B) Another animal, the ptarmigan, is an archtic bird that turns white in the winter to blend in with the snow. Some animals have caracteristics that mimick other objects as a form of protection. For example, walking-stick insects are shaped like twigs.

(C) Both passages have at least one spelling error.

---

7. **(A)** Sea turtles can grow to eight feet in length. They are excellant swimmers. Their legs are shaped like flippers, similer to the shape of oars, which make it tough for them to navigate the topograghy on land. Sea turtles are not as talented swimmers as dolfins.

(B) Some dolphins can swim at speeds of up to thirty-five miles per hour. Their skin has special streamlining modifications that allow them to swim so easily. They prupel themselves by flapping their tail fin up and down. Dolphins use sound waves, also known as sonar and echolocation, to navigate through their watery serroundings.

(C) Both passages have at least one spelling error.

---

8. **(A)** The grasshopper is so called because of its ability to leap. Its back legs are powerful. The femur of the male's back legs has a row of joints that stick out. When they are rubbed against the hard veins of the wings, the characteristic chirping sound is produced.

(B) Members of the grasshopper order include crickets and catydids. Another member, lochusts, are particulerly tough on farmers' crops. They feed veracioulsy on vegetation and lay their eggs in a small hole in the ground.

(C) Both passages have at least one spelling error.

Unit 6
Proofreading Strategy

Words with a silent consonant letter can be easily misspelled. Proofread carefully to make sure that words are spelled correctly.

wrinkle not *rinkle*

Words that contain the /ô/ sound can have a variety of spellings. Proofread carefully to make sure such words are spelled correctly.

fraud not *frawd*

Remember to use 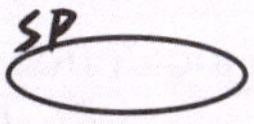 when you find a spelling error in your writing.

Read each passage. Choose *A* if only passage A has at least one spelling error. Choose *B* if only passage B has at least one spelling error. Choose *C* if both passages have at least one spelling error.

9. **(A)** In the late 1800s, a new type of stage show was launched in the United States. Similar to the English music haul, it was called vawdeville and included songs, dances, acrobatic shows, and comic skits. Magicians and jugglers would also entertain during these shows.

(B) Members of the audience, or spectators, would laugh or applaud to show that they enjoyed the show. A sure sine that the show was in trouble was when the audience began to yawn. By the late 1920s, however, the popularity of this kind of show began to decline as the motion picture industry developed. There was only halfhearted interest, and soon vaudeville was no more.

(C) Both passages have at least one spelling error.

---

10. **(A)** Windsor Castle is the largest occupied castle in the world. Located in the south of England on the Thames River, it is a site to see. It is one of the official residences of the queen. For nine hundred years, it has been a symbol of the rein of the monarcy. Visiters are free to tour the State Apartments, a vast set of rooms with beautifully designed decor.

(B) Within the castle are a host of other attractions. St. George's chapel is the burial place of ten sovereigns. It is also the site of many royal weddings, where many guests have let out sighs of satisfaction and tears of happiness. There was much hand wringing when the castle caught on fire in 1992. It took five years of exausting work and almost sixty million dollars to restore the castle to its former glory.

(C) Both passages have at least one spelling error.

Unit 6

Proofreading Strategy

Read each passage. Choose *A* if only passage A has at least one spelling error. Choose *B* if only passage B has at least one spelling error. Choose *C* if both passages have at least one spelling error.

11. **(A)** An almanac is a book or a pamphlet that is published once a year. It usually contains a lot of practicle information. Sometimes it offers interesting tidbits, such as why horses nay. It often includes a calendar; significant dates and events; and facts about governments, history, geography, and weather. Historical almanacs also included the movement of the planets, setting and rising times of the sun, and hi and low tides.

(B) Benjamin Franklin rote his own almanac, which he called *Poor Richard's Almanac*. Poor Richard was a fictitious character who didn't have a lot of scooling, although he was an intelligent philosofer. *Poor Richard's Almanac* was full of famous sayings such as "Haste makes waste." It also contained information on the phases of the moon. Of course, Franklin is famous for many other things, including demonstrating that litening is a form of electricity.

(C) Both passages have at least one spelling error.

---

12. **(A)** The human stomach is a baglike organ. It is shaped like the letter *J*. The mussles in the wall of this organ allow it to churn and mix the food contained within it. Sometimes we get a "not" in our stomachs, but it's usually because we're nervess about something—not the result of something we ate.

(B) The stomachs of some animals are different from those of humans. For example, the stomach of a cow—and of course, its offspring, the calf—has four chambers. The cow's stomach helps the cow to digest its primary source of nutrition—grass. Cattle ranchers pay close attention to what they feed their cattle because they don't want them to succumb to life-threatening diseases.

(C) Both passages have at least one spelling error.

13. **(A)** On January 20, following a presidential election in November, the next president is inaugurated in front of the United States Capitol in Washington, D.C. In this ceremony, the new president vows to be the protector and guardian of the Constitution of the United States. Millions of people, their interest piqued, watch the event on television. Thomas Jefferson, the third United States president, was the first president to have this ceremony in Washington, D.C.

(B) William Henry Harrison, the ninth president of the United States, gave the longest inauguration speech of any president. His speech was more than eight thousand words long! He gave his speech during retched weather—a furious snowstorm. He died of neumonia only one month later. Some say that the sixty-eight-year-old president contracted neumonia as a result of the fateeg caused by the early demands of the presidential office. Some also think that he caught a cold during his inaugural address, and that cold later turned to neumonia.

(C) Both passages have at least one spelling error.

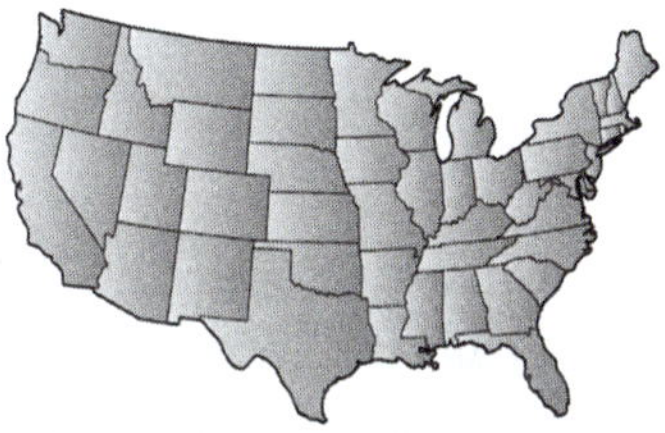

14. **(A)** The moon appears to change size and shape throughout the month. These changes are called the phases of the moon. The moon is illuminated by sunlite, and as the moon orbets Earth, we see different parts of its sunlit surface. The moon will change from a slim crescent to a full circle and back again. It orbets every twenty-seven days. The moon is uniche in that it is Earth's only satellite.

(B) The moon's origin is still debated. One theery is that the moon was formed from debree thrown off Earth when it was nocked with an enormous celestiel body. Regardless of its origin, the moon is vital, and it also provides humans with delite, especially during a luner eclipse. This occurs when the sun, Earth, and the moon aline. The moon passes into the shadow of Earth and is dim until it emurges from the shadow.

(C) Both passages have at least one spelling error.

Unit 6
Proofreading Strategy

Read each passage. Choose *A* if only passage A has at least one spelling error. Choose *B* if only passage B has at least one spelling error. Choose *C* if both passages have at least one spelling error.

15. **(A)** Roald Dahl was a famous British author. He wrote *Charlie and the Chocolate Factory* and *James and the Giant Peach.* He wrote about difficult subjects, such as death, with honesty. His extraordinary characters create a world that is fascinating to both children and adults. His books have been brought to life on the movie screen and on television.

(B) In *Charlie and the Choclate Factory,* Willy Wonka puts tickets in only a handful of his candy bars. The fortunate people who obtain these tickets are given a tour of Willy Wonka's factory. Everyone wants a ticket, and some people even ressle each other for the candy bars. In the story, Charlie is very poor and cannot spend a lot of money on candy. However, every time he opens a candy bar, he is hopeful. The dawter of a rich man gets a ticket because her father buys thousands of candy bars for his employees to unwrap.

(C) Both passages have at least one spelling error.

---

16. **(A)** Salmon is a fish that many people find delectible to eat. Most salmon are born in freshwater but spend the remainder of their lives in salt water. They do return to the freshwater to spaun, or reproduce, however. Salmon usually do this in the summer or autumn. They often have to overcome great obsticles, fighting currents and rapids, and even climing waterfalls. Salmon may spend up to four years at sea before returning to their home streams.

(B) A penguin is a flightless bird that spends most of its time in the ocean. Penguins are found in the southern hemisphere. They have thick feathers that insulate them from the frosty temperatures. Their walk, or waddle, seems awkward, but they are very graceful swimmers because their wings have evolved into flippers. Penguins also travel over land and ice by sliding on their bellies.

(C) Both passages have at least one spelling error.

17. **(A)** The guitar is a stringed instrument that can accompany singers, bands, or orchestras. Musicians can strum the strings to produce chords or simply pluck each string to produce individual notes. For many years, musicians played acoustic guitars, which produced sounds from the vibrations of the strings. Today, musicians can also play electric guitars, which produce sounds through electrical impulses and can be ampliphied.

(B) An orchestra is a group of musicians who play various instruments together. There are many different kinds of orchestras, depending on the type of instruments being played. Many African and Asian orchestras consist of only percussian instruments like drums, gongs, and xylophones. A symphony orchestra usually refers to an orchestra with mainly stringed instruments such as violins, violas, and cellos. This type of orchestra often accompanies operas and ballets.

(C) Both passages have at least one spelling error.

---

18. **(A)** Before there was currency, or money, people bartered in order to get the goods or services they wanted or needed. They would exchange cattle, animal hides, cloth, and salt for other indispensible items they needed from others. The first coins were probably made in a country called Lydia, now western Turkey. These coins were garanteed by the monarch of Lydia to have value. The last king of Lydia was conquered in 546 B.C.

(B) Eleanor Roosevelt was the wife of Franklin D. Roosevelt, a former president of the United States. However, Eleanor became a very influential figure in her own right. She was the mother of six children—five sons and one daughter. She often held press conferences for women reporters only and wrote her own daily newspaper colum, nown as "My Day." She fought for equal rights for minority groups and served as chair on the United Nations Commission on Human Rights.

(C) Both passages have at least one spelling error.

The Third LAP
Language Activity Pages

A. Exercising Your Skill

You have been learning about using a dictionary to help you spell words. You have also learned about the importance of proofreading your writing to check for misspelled words. Number your paper from 1 to 5. Answer the following questions about what you have learned.

1. Which of the following letter combinations can make the /f/ sound?
   (A) *qu, gh* **(B)** *ph, gh* **(C)** *ch, ph* **(D)** *ph, qu*

2. Which of the following letter combinations can make the /k/ sound?
   (A) *qu, gh* **(B)** *c, gh* **(C)** *ch, ph* **(D)** *qu, ch*

3. Which of the following words has a silent consonant?
   (A) scrape **(B)** consign **(C)** member **(D)** milk

4. Which group of suffixes means "capable of" or "tending to"?
   (A) *-able* and *-ible*
   (B) *-ence* and *-ance*

5. Which group of prefixes means "together"?
   (A) *en-*, *em-*, and *in-*
   (B) *con-*, *com-*, and *col-*
   (C) *ir-* and *il-*
   (D) *mis-* and *dis-*

B. Expanding Your Skill

Number your paper from 1 to 6. Read the paragraph below about the president of the United States. Practicing the proofreading strategy, find the misspelled words, and rewrite each word with its correct spelling. Use a dictionary if needed.

Setting the guidelines and limits of the position of president of the United States was a difficult task. The awthors of the Constitution wanted a strong leader but did not want him to be an all-powerful king. His duties begin on the day of inouguration, which is held on January 20th. He is the commandor in chief of the nation's armed forces. He is also responsable for developing relationships with forin countries. However, the United States Congress makes sure the president follows the laws set forth in the Constitution. If he does not, he may be inpeached.

C. Exploring Language

Poetry Read the limericks below written by Edward Lear. Number your paper from 1 to 5. For each number, correctly write each misspelled word from the limericks.

There was an Old Man with a beard,
Who said, 'It is just as I feared!
Two Owls and a Hen,
Four Larks and a Ren,
Have all built their nests in my beard!'

There was a Young Lady of Portugal,
Whose ideas were excessevely nawtical:
She climed up a tree,
To examine the sea,
But declared she would never leave Portugal.

There was a Young Lady whose eyes,
Were unlike as to color and size;
When she opened them wide,
People all turned aside,
And started away in surprize.

D. Expressing Yourself

Choose one of these activities. When you are finished, give your paper to your teacher.

1. WORK with a PARTNER Write a paragraph in which you purposely misspell at least five words that use the spelling patterns you have just learned. For example, you may misspell the word *flight* by taking out the silent letters *gh*, and adding an *e* to form *flite*. When you are finished, exchange your paper with your partner. Proofread your partner's paragraph, and correct the misspellings you find. Your partner will do the same. Exchange papers again to check one another's corrections.

2. The United States has had a total of forty-three presidents. Use an encyclopedia or other resources to look up a president of your choice. Read the information carefully, and make a list of words that begin with *con-*, *col-*, or *com-*. Then make a list of words that end with *-ion, -ible, -able, -ance,* or *-ence.*

Unit 7

Family Strategy

Matching words with their base words will help you learn how to spell words with added endings. A base word can have different prefixes, suffixes, and endings added to form related words.

critic → critic<u>al</u> → critic<u>ize</u>

When endings are added to base words, sometimes a vowel sound can change. In most vowel-sound changes, only the sound changes while the letter remains the same.

m<u>a</u>jor → m<u>a</u>jority (The *a* in *major* is the /ā/ sound, and the *a* in *majority* is the /ə/ sound.)

Choose the word that does *not* belong in the same family as the other three words.

1. **(A)** discourage **(B)** encouragement **(C)** courtesy **(D)** courageous

2. **(A)** immature **(B)** mature **(C)** prematurely **(D)** miniature

3. **(A)** separate **(B)** partition **(C)** inseparable **(D)** separation

4. **(A)** nectar **(B)** necessary **(C)** necessitate **(D)** unnecessarily

5. **(A)** behave **(B)** misbehave **(C)** behavior **(D)** havoc

6. **(A)** mislead **(B)** leadership **(C)** ladder **(D)** leader

7. **(A)** indirect **(B)** direction **(C)** misdirect **(D)** direness

8. **(A)** impolite **(B)** elite **(C)** polite **(D)** politely

9. **(A)** inspection **(B)** disrespect **(C)** respectable **(D)** respect

10. **(A)** recess **(B)** recession **(C)** recessive **(D)** receivable

11. **(A)** contain **(B)** containment **(C)** contaminate **(D)** container

12. **(A)** consequently **(B)** quenchable **(C)** consequential **(D)** consequence

13. **(A)** collection **(B)** collector **(C)** collision **(D)** recollect

14. **(A)** musician **(B)** musical **(C)** musty **(D)** music

15. **(A)** add **(B)** addition **(C)** additive **(D)** adaptable

16. **(A)** divulge **(B)** divide **(C)** divisive **(D)** indivisible

17. **(A)** kindness **(B)** unkind **(C)** kindergarten **(D)** kind

18. **(A)** human **(B)** humane **(C)** humanity **(D)** humble

19. **(A)** assert **(B)** assertive **(C)** dessert **(D)** assertion

20. **(A)** abort **(B)** able **(C)** ability **(D)** disable

Unit 7

Family Strategy

Choose the correct base word for each underlined word.

21. Space exploration is how humans learn more about Earth, the moon, the planets, and the stars.
(A) explore **(B)** extra **(C)** explanation **(D)** explorative

22. Astronauts have to go through a considerable amount of training.
(A) consideration **(B)** inconsiderate **(C)** consider **(D)** insider

23. Space vehicles have a combination of oxygen and nitrogen for the astronauts to breathe.
(A) combined **(B)** combine **(C)** comb **(D)** combust

24. On a space shuttle, a fuel cell generates electricity for the space vehicle.
(A) electrician **(B)** electrical **(C)** elect **(D)** electric

25. Astronauts see some of the most amazing sights imaginable.
(A) imagine **(B)** imagination **(C)** magazine **(D)** margin

26. Many people find the work of astronauts admirable.
(A) admiration **(B)** admire **(C)** miracle **(D)** admission

27. Astronauts must go through rigorous training.
(A) rigor **(B)** rigid **(C)** rig **(D)** rigidity

28. Astronauts have assorted duties.
(A) consort **(B)** assort **(C)** sortable **(D)** resort

29. On one mission, the crew's goal was to make reparations to the Hubble Space Telescope.
(A) repair **(B)** prepare **(C)** pare **(D)** preparation

30. The Hubble was originally placed in orbit around Earth in 1990.
(A) organ **(B)** origin **(C)** original **(D)** organize

31. Much to the dismay of NASA, it was discovered that the Hubble was not working properly.
(A) prop **(B)** proper **(C)** improper **(D)** propel

32. It needed corrective optical devices in order to focus.
(A) correct **(B)** incorrect **(C)** correction **(D)** correlate

Unit 7
Family Strategy

33. If there were no light, then seeing would be impossible.
(A) possibility **(B)** imposter **(C)** possible **(D)** possession

34. Light is emitted naturally from the sun and the stars.
(A) natural **(B)** nature **(C)** unnaturally **(D)** natal

35. Sir Isaac Newton discovered that white light is made of all the colors.
(A) discover **(B)** discovery **(C)** undiscovered **(D)** hover

36. White light can be separated through a prism into a continuous spectrum of colors.
(A) continuity **(B)** continue **(C)** continual **(D)** continent

37. The speed of light is invariant, which means the speed of light never changes.
(A) vary **(B)** variable **(C)** varying **(D)** invariable

38. The speed of light was first measured accurately by Olaus Roemer.
(A) accuracy **(B)** accurate **(C)** cure **(D)** inaccurate

39. Roemer was a Danish astronomer who lived in the 1600s.
(A) astro **(B)** astronomical **(C)** astronomy **(D)** astrology

40. Light travels remarkably fast—186,000 miles per second.
(A) mark **(B)** market **(C)** unremarkable **(D)** remarkable

41. In comparison, sound travels much more slowly.
(A) comparable **(B)** incomparable **(C)** compare **(D)** pare

42. Sound is a sensation received by the ear through vibrations.
(A) vibrant **(B)** viable **(C)** vibrate **(D)** vibrating

43. The speed at which a sound wave travels is dependent on the temperature.
(A) pending **(B)** depending **(C)** independent **(D)** depend

44. Carefully designed aircraft of today can travel faster than the speed of sound.
(A) uncaring **(B)** careless **(C)** care **(D)** cared

Unit 7
Family Strategy

Which word has a vowel sound change from its given base word?

45. decide
(A) decisive (B) decision (C) deciding

46. collide
(A) colliding (B) collided (C) collision

47. inquire
(A) inquisitive (B) inquiring (C) inquired

48. explain
(A) explaining (B) explanation (C) explained

49. perspire
(A) perspiration (B) perspiring (C) perspired

50. relate
(A) related (B) relative (C) relation

51. exclaim
(A) exclamatory (B) exclaimed (C) exclaiming

52. admire
(A) admiring (B) admiration (C) admired

53. produce
(A) productivity (B) producer (C) producing

54. reveal
(A) revealer (B) revelation (C) revealing

55. incline
(A) inclining (B) incliner (C) inclination

Unit 7
Family Strategy

56. solid
(A) solidly **(B)** solidify **(C)** solidarity

57. sane
(A) sanity **(B)** insane **(C)** saneness

58. restore
(A) restoring **(B)** restoration **(C)** restored

59. revise
(A) revision **(B)** revising **(C)** revised

60. reside
(A) resided **(B)** residing **(C)** resident

61. negate
(A) negated **(B)** negative **(C)** negating

62. ignite
(A) ignition **(B)** ignited **(C)** ignites

63. condense
(A) condensed **(B)** condensation **(C)** condensing

64. refer
(A) referee **(B)** referred **(C)** refers

65. meter
(A) centimeter **(B)** decimeter **(C)** metric

Unit 8

Foreign Language Strategy

Many English words are based on words from the Greek and Latin languages. They are called **Greek** or **Latin roots.** Each root has a specific meaning and usually combines with other words. Words with Greek and Latin roots are easier to spell and understand when broken into their parts.

Greek

bio = "life" ⟶ **bio**logy
chron = "time" ⟶ **chron**icle
cycl = "circle" ⟶ bi**cycl**e
graph = "writing" ⟶ auto**graph**
hydr = "water" ⟶ **hydr**ant
meter = "measure" ⟶ centi**meter**
ology = "study of" ⟶ psych**ology**
path = "disease" ⟶ sym**pathy**

Latin

aqua = "water" ⟶ **aqua**rium
aud = "hear" ⟶ **aud**ience
nat = "born" ⟶ **nat**ive
ped = "foot" ⟶ **ped**estrian
port = "carry" ⟶ **port**able
scrib, script = "write" ⟶ **scrib**e
vid, vis = "see" ⟶ **vid**eo

Which word part goes in the blank to correctly spell the word that makes sense in each sentence?

1. _____logy, or the study of living organisms, involves examination of animals and plants.
   (A) Cardo **(B)** Bio **(C)** Nato

2. A doctor may perform a _____psy to take a closer look at the living tissue of a person.
   (A) cyclo **(B)** bio **(C)** nato

3. A _____ge uses his or her knowledge of the law to oversee a trial.
   (A) min **(B)** ped **(C)** jud

4. Humans are bi _____; we walk on two feet.
   (A) cycles **(B)** forms **(C)** peds

5. A preacher cites _____ure while giving a sermon.
   (A) script **(B)** bio **(C)** audi

6. The word *geo*_____ literally means "earth measurement."
   (A) *graph* **(B)** *logy* **(C)** *metry*

Unit 8
Foreign Language Strategy

7. A ______one is a storm known for the circular shape it takes.
(A) hydr (B) cycl (C) graph

8. News reporters usually tell stories ______ologically, or in the order of what happened first.
(A) port (B) path (C) chron

9. A ______y uses its interpretation of evidence to decide a trial's verdict.
(A) min (B) ped (C) jur

10. Trucks trans______ products across the country.
(A) aud (B) port (C) flect

11. ______imum wage is the lowest wage allowed by law for a worker.
(A) Aud (B) Min (C) Card

12. Someone who is ______ible can bend and stretch very easily.
(A) port (B) flex (C) ped

13. A pregnant woman takes pre______al vitamins to keep her unborn baby healthy.
(A) form (B) cycl (C) nat

14. Architects rely on ______ual aids to allow people to see their designs.
(A) script (B) vis (C) form

15. Certain pieces of orchestral music are played so that they are barely ______ible.
(A) aud (B) vis (C) flex

16. People in the army wear uni______s.
(A) form (B) port (C) volve

17. A re______r is a gun with a barrel that turns.
(A) flect (B) graph (C) volve

18. A bio______y is a book written about someone's life.
(A) graph (B) card (C) path

Unit 8
Foreign Language Strategy

Which word part goes in the blank to correctly spell the word that makes sense in each sentence?

19. Re_____ion is a turning inward to think about things.
(A) port **(B)** flect **(C)** flex

20. A _____ologist studies diseases and their causes.
(A) chron **(B)** path **(C)** nat

21. People who exercise must stay _____ated
(A) form **(B)** hydr **(C)** graph

22. There are a total of nine _____tices who serve on the Supreme Court.
(A) jur **(B)** jud **(C)** jus

23. The goalie in a hockey game de_____s, or turns away, the puck from the goal.
(A) ped **(B)** volve **(C)** flect

24. After days of tests and cultures, the doctor finally wrote a pre_____ion.
(A) scrib **(B)** port **(C)** script

25. It's important to re_____ waste so it can be used again.
(A) form **(B)** port **(C)** cycle

26. An in_____e talent is one you are born with.
(A) cycl **(B)** volv **(C)** nat

27. A tran_____ in a trial is a written record of what was said.
(A) script **(B)** card **(C)** graph

28. Children are sometimes _____iature versions of their parents.
(A) aud **(B)** nat **(C)** min

29. Many people genu_____, or bend at the knee, at a place of worship.
(A) flect **(B)** ped **(C)** port

30. As their ideas took shape, the scientists began to _____ulate a question.
(A) path **(B)** aud **(C)** form

Unit 8
Foreign Language Strategy

Each sentence below includes a word with a Greek or Latin root. Which sentence does *not* have a spelling error?

31. **(A)** The doctor was a specialist in kardiology.
(B) The man had a cardiogram to see if his heart was in good shape.

32. **(A)** A sympethetic person shows kind feelings toward other people.
(B) Empathy is not the same as sympathy.

33. **(A)** A hydraulic tool uses water or other liquid to help increase efficiency.
(B) A hidroelectric power plant uses the power of water to create electricity.

34. **(A)** Someone who is gregarious likes to be with people.
(B) A church relies on its congrigation for support.

35. **(A)** A thermomiter is an instrument that measures temperature.
(B) A barometer measures the pressure in the atmosphere.

36. **(A)** Usually, historians relate an important event in kronological order.
(B) A chronology is the arrangement of events based on the order in which they occurred.

37. **(A)** Not long ago, schools were segregated by race.
(B) Civil rights activists fought hard to bring about desegrigation of schools.

38. **(A)** The justice system is not perfect.
(B) Judments become public record.

39. **(A)** The seasons are sicklicle.
(B) Performers sometimes ride unicycles.

40. **(A)** Most high schools have auditoriums where students gather to listen to speakers.
(B) A dog whistle is inawdible to the human ear.

41. **(A)** The center of a pencil is made of grafite.
(B) A phonograph, used to play records, was once a very popular device.

42. **(A)** Someone with empathy can imagine what another person is feeling.
(B) A pathalogical liar is someone who has a lying "disease."

Unit 8

Foreign Language Strategy

Many English words come from the German and French languages. Instead of borrowing root words with specific meanings, the English language adopted some of their spelling patterns.

German words often have the /ûr/ sound spelled *er* and *ur,* the /əl/ sound spelled *el;* the /ou/ sound spelled *au* or *ow,* and the /ē/ sound spelled *ie.*

ham**burger** pret**zel** kr**au**t ch**ow**der sp**ie**l

French words often have the /ā/ sound spelled *e, ee, et* (*t* is silent), and *ai;* the /k/ sound spelled *qu;* and the /o͞o/ sound spelled *ou.*

caf**é** chal**et** mayonn**ai**se bouti**que** r**ou**lette

Choose the sentence with the underlined word that is spelled correctly.

43. **(A)** An entrée is the main dish served at a meal.
 (B) An entre is the main dish served at a meal.

44. **(A)** A bride usually carries a beautiful bouqai of flowers.
 (B) A bride usually carries a beautiful bouquet of flowers.

45. **(A)** A locomotive has a diesel engine.
 (B) A locomotive has a deesel engine.

46. **(A)** The word *kindergarten* means "garden of children."
 (B) The word *kindurgarten* means "garden of children."

47. **(A)** A parfait is a layered treat.
 (B) A parfet is a layered treat.

48. **(A)** The hamstur is a small rodent.
 (B) The hamster is a small rodent.

49. **(A)** The American hot dog is similar to a frankfurter.
 (B) The American hot dog is similar to a frankferter.

50. **(A)** Liverwurst is sold at most supermarkets.
 (B) Liverwerst is sold at most supermarkets.

51. **(A)** Some people put sauerkrowt on their hot dogs.
 (B) Some people put sauerkraut on their hot dogs.

52. **(A)** Strudel is a sweet pastry.
 (B) Strudle is a sweet pastry.

Unit 8

Foreign Language Strategy

53. **(A)** Hollywood Bullevard is one of the best-known streets in California.
    (B) Hollywood Boulevard is one of the best-known streets in California.

54. **(A)** A bisque is a thick soup that is sometimes made of cooked shellfish.
    (B) A bisk is a thick soup that is sometimes made of cooked shellfish.

55. **(A)** Pumpurnickil is a dark bread made from coarse, whole rye.
    (B) Pumpernickel is a dark bread made from coarse, whole rye.

56. **(A)** The man's fiancée searched everywhere for a bridal gown.
    (B) The man's fiancet searched everywhere for a bridal gown.

57. **(A)** Tourists travel to the warm waters of Florida to snorkel in the ocean.
    (B) Tourists travel to the warm waters of Florida to snorkil in the ocean.

58. **(A)** The travelers took a deture around the construction site.
    (B) The travelers took a detour around the construction site.

59. **(A)** A seashell is a great suvenir to take home from the beach.
    (B) A seashell is a great souvenir to take home from the beach.

60. **(A)** The gourmet chef had his own television show.
    (B) The gourmes chef had his own television show.

61. **(A)** The résumét is on the desk.
    (B) The résumé is on the desk.

62. **(A)** The construction worker complained of migrane headaches.
    (B) The construction worker complained of migraine headaches.

63. **(A)** Bodybuilders have excellent physikes.
    (B) Bodybuilders have excellent physiques.

64. **(A)** An appliqué is a decoration you fasten to a larger piece of material.
    (B) An appliquai is a decoration you fasten to a larger piece of material.

Unit 8

Foreign Language Strategy

Many words in the English language have also adopted spelling patterns from the Italian and Spanish languages. Many Italian and Spanish words end with a vowel. In most cases, when a word ends in the /ə/ sound, it is spelled with an *a*. In Italian, when the word ends in the /ē/ sound, it is usually spelled with an *i*.

Italian: lasagn**a**; pepperon**i**

Spanish: mes**a**; bronc**o**

Many Spanish and Italian words contain double consonants.

Italian: ce**ll**o

Spanish: torti**ll**a

Choose the sentence with the underlined word that is spelled correctly.

65. **(A)** Alfalfa is a deep-rooted plant used for hay.
(B) Alfalfe is a deep-rooted plant used for hay.

66. **(A)** Spaghetti is a favorite food of many.
(B) Spagheti is a favorite food of many.

67. **(A)** In Mexico, large farms are called haciendhus.
(B) In Mexico, large farms are called haciendas.

68. **(A)** During a fieste, people dance, have parades, and ring bells.
(B) During a fiesta, people dance, have parades, and ring bells.

69. **(A)** A coral is a fenced area where horses and other animals are gathered together.
(B) A corral is a fenced area where horses and other animals are gathered together.

70. **(A)** A gondola is both a long, narrow boat and the basket that hangs from a balloon.
(B) A gondole is both a long, narrow boat and the basket that hangs from a balloon.

71. **(A)** What do you like on your piza?
(B) What do you like on your pizza?

72. **(A)** A burrow is a small donkey.
(B) A burro is a small donkey.

Unit 8
Foreign Language Strategy

73. **(A)** Some women apply mascare to their eyelashes to make them look longer.
(B) Some women apply mascara to their eyelashes to make them look longer.

74. **(A)** A plazza is a public square in a city or a town.
(B) A plaza is a public square in a city or a town.

75. **(A)** The word *mosquitoh* means "little fly."
(B) The word *mosquito* means "little fly."

76. **(A)** A person who is incognito is wearing a disguise and does not want to be recognized.
(B) A person who is incognitto is wearing a disguise and does not want to be recognized.

77. **(A)** Stiletto heels are very thin, high, and pointy.
(B) Stileto heels are very thin, high, and pointy.

78. **(A)** Macoronee and cheese is a favorite American side dish.
(B) Macaroni and cheese is a favorite American side dish.

79. **(A)** People like to throw confettee at parades.
(B) People like to throw confetti at parades.

80. **(A)** *Mañana* means "tomorrow" in Spanish.
(B) *Mañane* means "tomorrow" in Spanish.

81. **(A)** A siera is a range of mountains with an irregular outline.
(B) A sierra is a range of mountains with an irregular outline.

82. **(A)** Stucko is a fine plaster used in decorations and on walls.
(B) Stucco is a fine plaster used in decorations and on walls.

The Last LAP
Language Activity Pages

A. Exercising Your Skill

You have been learning about spelling words using the family strategy and the foreign language strategy. Number your paper from 1 to 4. Answer the following questions about what you have learned.

1. When you add a suffix to a base word, which of the following is true?
   (A) The vowels within the base word usually change.
   (B) The sounds of the vowels within the base word always change.
   (C) The vowels within the base word usually stay the same, even if the sound changes.

2. Which of the following is true of words borrowed from Italian and Spanish?
   (A) They always end in a vowel.
   (B) Many have double consonants.
   (C) The letter *a* at the end of a word is usually pronounced /ā/.

3. Which of the following word pairs contain the same Greek or Latin root, with the same meaning?
   (A) visual, video
   (B) audience, awful
   (C) pedestrian, loped

4. Which of the following word pairs contain the same Greek or Latin root?
   (A) natural, gnat
   (B) jury, judicial
   (C) vermin, minimum

B. Expanding Your Skill

Number your paper from 1 to 4. Write the letter of the root that correctly completes each word on your paper.

1. The guilty verdict did not di______ish the family's grief.
   (A) form **(B)** min **(C)** flect

2. A system or body of law is called ______isprudence.
   (A) vid **(B)** port **(C)** jur

3. Syn______ized swimmers perform the same movements at the same time.
   (A) form **(B)** chron **(C)** greg

4. A psycho______ is someone who has a diseased mind.
   (A) ped **(B)** graph **(C)** path

C. Exploring Language

Poetry Every day we use words with Greek and Latin roots and words with French, German, Italian, and Spanish spelling patterns. Read the silly poem below about the English language. Number your paper from 1 to 8. Choose the word from the box that correctly completes each line of the poem.

uniform	script	evolves	cycles
pepperoni	pedestrian	autograph	reflection

English is a **(1)** _____ of many different tongues
Without our beloved words, we would all be struck dumb!
A movie star gives fans her **(2)** _____—she doesn't need to speak.
But without a **(3)** _____ to read, she might just give a shriek.
A **(4)** _____ wouldn't know what to call himself as he runs across a street.
Eating bologna, salami, **(5)** _____, and other yummy meats.
Our language has a taste of different cultures—it's not **(6)** _____ at all,
From one year to the next, it goes through **(7)**_____ and **(8)**_____.

D. Expressing Yourself

Choose one of these activities. When you are finished, give your paper to your teacher.

1. Look at the list of words below and determine from which language the word originated. Write your answers on a separate sheet of paper, and then use the word in a complete sentence. Use a dictionary if you need help with any of the word meanings.

polka	saxophone	bizarre
alfresco	perform	palomino

2. **WORK with a PARTNER** Write a silly story that is a few paragraphs long. Try to include words you know that come from a language other than English. When you are finished, circle ten of the words you used. On another paper, write down the languages the words came from; use a dictionary. Exchange your story with your partner. See if you can figure out where your partner's circled words came from *without* using a dictionary. Then discuss your answers with your partner.

SPELLING Scope and Sequence • *Specific Skill Series for Language Arts*

Unit/Level	Level A	Level B	Level C	Level D	Level E	Level F	Level G	Level H
Unit 1	Pronunciation Strategy	Pronunciation Strategy	Pronunciation Strategy	Rhyming Strategy	Rhyming Strategy	Conventions Strategy	Conventions Strategy	Conventions Strategy
Unit 2	Pronunciation Strategy	Pronunciation Strategy	Pronunciation Strategy	Conventions Strategy	Conventions Strategy	Visualization Strategy	Visualization Strategy	Visualization Strategy
Unit 3	Pronunciation Strategy	Pronunciation Strategy	Pronunciation Strategy	Conventions Strategy	Visualization Strategy	Visualization Strategy	Visualization Strategy	Visualization Strategy
Unit 4	Visualization Strategy	Pronunciation Strategy	Rhyming Strategy	Visualization Strategy	Visualization Strategy	Meaning Strategy	Meaning Strategy	Meaning Strategy
Unit 5	Visualization Strategy	Vowel Substitution Strategy	Rhyming Strategy	Visualization Strategy	Compound Word Strategy	Dictionary Strategy	Dictionary Strategy	Dictionary Strategy
Unit 6	Visualization Strategy	Vowel Substitution Strategy	Conventions Strategy	Visualization Strategy	Meaning Strategy	Proofreading Strategy	Proofreading Strategy	Proofreading Strategy
Unit 7	Consonant Substitution Strategy	Consonant Substitution Strategy	Conventions Strategy	Compound Word Strategy	Dictionary Strategy	Family Strategy	Family Strategy	Family Strategy
Unit 8	Vowel Substitution Strategy	Rhyming Strategy	Visualization Strategy	Meaning Strategy	Proofreading Strategy	Foreign Language Strategy	Foreign Language Strategy	Foreign Language Strategy
Unit 9	Rhyming Strategy	Rhyming Strategy	Visualization Strategy	Dictionary Strategy	Family Strategy			
Unit 10	Rhyming Strategy	Conventions Strategy	Visualization Strategy	Proofreading Strategy	Foreign Language Strategy			
Unit 11	Conventions Strategy	Conventions Strategy	Compound Word Strategy	Family Strategy				
Unit 12	Conventions Strategy	Conventions Strategy	Meaning Strategy	Foreign Language Strategy				
Unit 13		Compound Word Strategy	Dictionary Strategy					
Unit 14		Meaning Strategy	Family Strategy					
Unit 15			Family Strategy					